Harry Potter

DOBBY

A Behind-the-Scenes Look at the House-Elves of the Harry Potter Films

By Jody Revenson

INCREDI
BUILDS

A Division of Insight Editions, LP
San Rafael, California

INTRODUCTION

A house-elf is required to serve one wizarding family for their entire life, and house-elves are very faithful to their masters. Any command their master gives them must be obeyed, though it helps to be specific, because a house-elf may not perform the order exactly as it was meant to be done! When house-elves don't follow instructions, or say something bad about their master, they are forced to punish themselves. Although house-elves are small, they can actually perform incredibly powerful magic – and without the use of a wand! Since house-elves can only be released from their slavery by a gift from their master of a piece of clothing, they often wear a filthy discarded tea towel or pillowcase.

A WELL-LOVED CHARACTER

Dobby's first appearance in the Harry Potter films was in *Harry Potter and the Chamber of Secrets*, when the house-elf is discovered in Harry's bedroom at the Dursleys'. Dobby is trying to keep Harry from going back to Hogwarts, where he may be harmed. Dobby was already a big favourite of readers, so it was important that when he was brought to life on-screen, he would be just as beloved.

DOBBY DECISIONS

The director of *Harry Potter and the Chamber of Secrets*, Chris Columbus, wanted to make sure that Dobby would feel very real. At first, the filmmakers thought that Dobby could be a puppet that would be operated on set, making it easier for the actors to interact with him. But it was soon decided that Dobby would become the film series' first fully computer-generated major character.

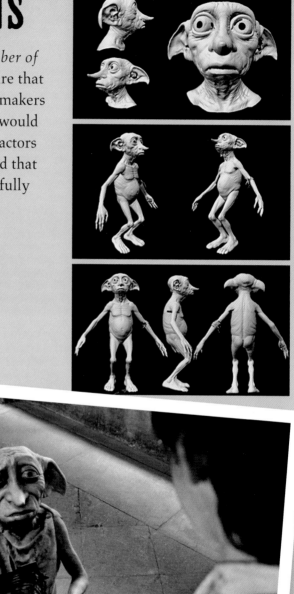

LOOK HERE!

Because Dobby wouldn't physically interact with Harry Potter or other characters on the film set, the filmmakers used a tennis ball on a stick in his place. This is a long-used method that allows actors to focus on where the character should be. It also provides the computer animators with a visual reference for where to place the character within the scene.

EYES ON THE BALL

Chris Columbus, director of *Chamber of Secrets*, knew that it would be a challenge to direct Daniel Radcliffe's (Harry Potter) scenes when he interacts with Dobby. "He wouldn't have anyone in the room to act with," says Chris. "He was basically acting with a little green tennis ball! But Daniel was so focused he made you believe that Dobby was there."

CREATING DOBBY'S LOOK

CGI, which stands for 'computer-generated imagery', involves many steps between coming up with the design of the character and putting that character on screen. The process for Dobby started with ideas for what the house-elf would look like, which were drawn by visual development artists. Dobby went through many design ideas before the big-eyed, bat-eared, pointy-nosed house-elf emerged. The artists also thought about Dobby's background as a servant to the Malfoy family, and so he was given a grey, pale 'prisoner of war' appearance, with grimy skin and little or no muscles.

"Master has given Dobby a sock! Master has presented Dobby with clothes! Dobby is free!"

—DOBBY, HARRY POTTER AND THE CHAMBER OF SECRETS FILM

A MODEL HOUSE-ELF

Once Dobby's look was established, the creature shop, headed by Nick Dudman, created a full-size three-dimensional model made out of silicon. The model had a metal skeleton inside so that its joints could be placed in any position. Then they made a few more models of Dobby in exactly the same way. Each model was fully painted, with lots and lots of details, right down to the veins in his eyes and the wrinkles on his skin. "Dobby's pasty and pale and covered with dirt and dressed in a rag," says Nick. "It may be an awful lot of work that needed to be done, but I think Dobby is a bit more real because we went through this process."

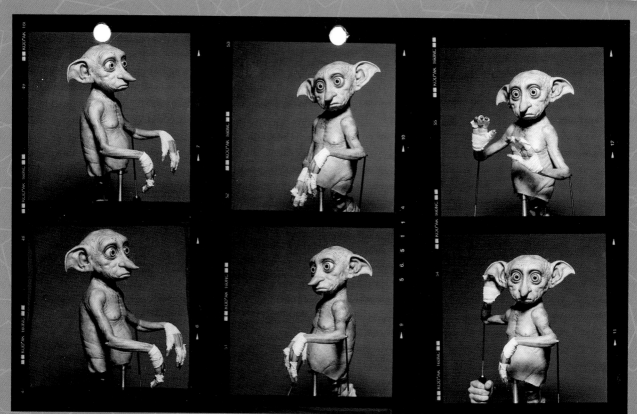

DOBBY ON SET

The life-size model of Dobby with the completely functioning armature inside was occasionally posed on the set before a scene was filmed. This helped the actors to know the specific place to look where Dobby would be and for the lighting designers to ensure that Dobby's lighting would be correct on the set. Then the model would be taken away, and the scene would be filmed with just the human actors. Dobby would be placed back into the scene by the animation team.

MODEL HOME

One of the life-size Dobby models used in the filming of *Harry Potter and the Chamber of Secrets* sits in the office of director Chris Columbus. "He guards the office for me," says Chris. "We did use the model for some over-the-shoulder shots in the film but Dobby was always going to be a CGI character, and I'm very proud of how he turned out." Another Dobby model was gifted by the author to a building in Aberdeen, Scotland, that became a cinema.

FACIAL EXPRESSIONS

Dobby's movement for *Harry Potter and the Chamber of Secrets* was achieved completely within the computer. However, actor Toby Jones, who performed the voice of the house-elf, would first act out Dobby's scenes for the animators. His facial expressions and physical movements would inspire the digital performance created by the computer-effects team. The animators did add one facial expression of their own, though: Dobby's smile always turns up on the left side of his mouth whether or not he is facing that way on-screen.

PROPS TO THE CGI TEAM

When Dobby tries to punish himself in *Harry Potter and the Chamber of Secrets* by banging his head with a lamp in Harry's bedroom, the scene was originally filmed with the real props needed on Harry's desk: a pencil holder, a photo album, a glass of water and a lamp. Then the filmmakers realised that Dobby was the one who was actually interacting with the props, so the special-effects team erased the originals in the film and replaced them with computer-animated versions.

VERY SPECIAL EFFECTS

In addition to Dobby and the props used in Harry's bedroom in *Chamber of Secrets*, the special-effects team also needed to create his shadow on the walls as he bounced around the room and the tears on his face when he cried.

PIECE OF CAKE

It was a computer-generated cake that floated across the room when Dobby snapped his fingers to send it in the direction of the Dursleys' guests at the beginning of *Harry Potter and the Chamber of Secrets*, but it was a real cake with whipped cream and sugared violets that fell onto Mrs Mason's head!

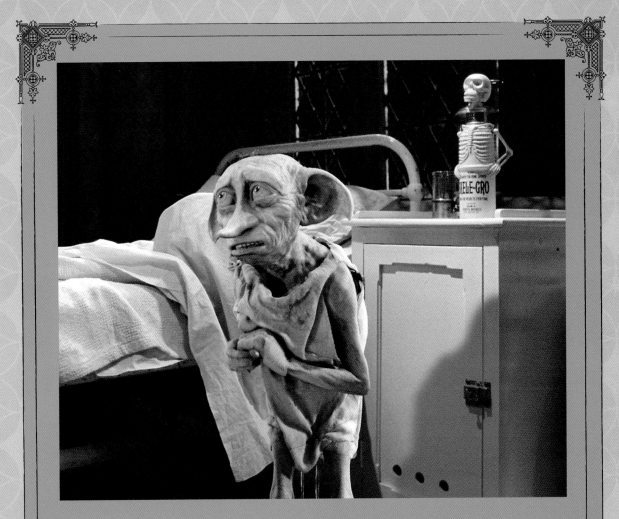

A MOVING HOUSE-ELF

For *Harry Potter and the Chamber of Secrets*, the computer-animation team wanted to ensure that Dobby always stood or moved like a house-elf who had been treated badly by his wizarding family for years. Very often, Dobby would wrap his arms around himself or curl inwards so that he could protect his body and be a smaller target. After Dobby is freed, his posture changes and he walks much taller and straighter.

UCIUS MALFOY AND DOBBY

on Isaacs, who played Lucius Malfoy in the
Potter films, acting alongside Dobby was a
of learning to believe in the unseen. "The
me I worked with Dobby," he says, "I asked,
where is Dobby going to be in the room?
re should I look?' I was told, 'Well, wherever
you look, that's where we'll put him!'"

"*Dobby is used to
death threats, sir.
Dobby gets them five
times a day at home.*"
– DOBBY, HARRY POTTER AND
THE CHAMBER OF SECRETS FILM

A LOST HOUSE-ELF

Winky is a female house-elf in the book *Harry Potter and the Goblet of Fire* who Harry meets at the Quidditch World Cup. The visual-development artists illustrated ideas of what she would look like, but unfortunately the character did not make it into the film.

KREACHER

"Kreacher lives to serve the Noble House of Black."
– KREACHER, HARRY POTTER AND THE ORDER OF THE PHOENIX FILM

Kreacher, who we first meet in *Harry Potter and the Order of the Phoenix*, is the house-elf for the Black family but he despises his current master, Sirius Black. Where Dobby is very likeable and energetic, Kreacher is the complete opposite. Kreacher moves slowly, acts slowly and does both with a noticeable grumble.

TOUJOURS ✴ PUR ✴

An Awful House Elf

"Yes, he's awful," laughs Nick Dudman, head of the creature shop. "He's the Black family's aged, crumbly retainer. And he hates everybody who isn't a pure-blood wizard – his loyalties are very much on the dark side." Nick wanted to make the nasty house-elf as revolting and ghastly in every way possible. "His ears droop much, much more than Dobby's, he's flappy all over, he's bent over with age and he barely moves when he walks."

AN UNMOVING HOUSE-ELF

The animators who work on a film usually create CGI characters that can fly, like Buckbeak, the Hippogriff in *Harry Potter and the Prisoner of Azkaban*, or swim, like the Grindylows in *Harry Potter and the Goblet of Fire*. To create Kreacher they had to go against their usual instincts in order to bring the elderly, bile-spewing house-elf to life. They created a performance with very little movement, deciding that at Kreacher's age, the character would, of course, walk slowly. Kreacher almost skulks, and always seems to be creeping up on people, which makes him all the more unappealing.

KREACHER'S VOICE

Kreacher was voiced by Timothy Bateson for *Order of the Phoenix*, then by Simon McBurney for *Harry Potter and the Deathly Hallows – Part 1*. Just like Toby Jones for Dobby, these actors' voice performances were filmed, but it was up to the animators to create the old house-elf's plodding movements and facial expressions.

EARS TO YOU

The designers had fun creating Kreacher's aged, collapsing skin, which was appropriately soft and stretchy for such an elderly character. They also gave him long, dragging ears complete with ear hair, and a little hair on his head, unlike Dobby. Kreacher was given a noticeable hunchbacked posture, a dewlap under his chin, watery eyes and a stooped stance that really portrayed disgust and intolerance.

BEHIND THE CURTAIN

Kreacher is seen cleaning and talking to a muttering curtain-covered portrait in the hallway of 12 Grimmauld Place in *Harry Potter and the Order of the Phoenix*. The painting is that of Sirius's mother, Walburga.

"Nasty brat standing there as bold as brass. Harry Potter, the boy who stopped the Dark Lord. Friend of Mudbloods and blood-traitors alike. If my poor mistress only knew..."

— KREACHER, *HARRY POTTER AND THE ORDER OF THE PHOENIX* FILM

PERFORMANCE ARTIST

Actor Timothy Bateson, Kreacher's voice in *Harry Potter and the Order of the Phoenix*, was filmed as he sat in a chair and read his lines and the team used his facial expressions and mannerisms as a performance reference. The actual combination of body language, attitude, how Kreacher moved around and how he reacted to Harry was entirely the creation of the animation team, who were proud that Kreacher was thought of as no less than a living being.

THE HOUSE-ELVES OF GRIMMAULD PLACE

In *Harry Potter and the Order of the Phoenix,* Harry observes a curious practice during his first visit to 12 Grimmauld Place, Sirius Black's family home and the headquarters of the Order of the Phoenix. Placed around the staircase to the second floor the heads of the former house-elves for the Black family are preserved and displayed in tall glass bell jars.

HEAD DESIGNER

Each ancient house-elf in the Black house had distinctive hair, teeth and snouts. Unlike the bald Dobby and the nearly bald Kreacher, these house-elves were given unique hairstyles. Visual-development artist Rob Bliss also explored different hats and collars for the house-elves, which help indicate the time period during which they served the family.

HOUSE-ELF ARMOUR

When writing a film, the filmmakers explore many ideas but not all of them make it to the final film. For *Harry Potter and the Half-Blood Prince*, it was proposed that armoured house-elf statues in the entrance hall stairway of Hogwarts would come to life by digital animation. Although the visual-development artists put these ideas on paper, they didn't make it into the film.

CO-CREATURES

In *Harry Potter and the Deathly Hallows – Part 1*, Harry, Ron and Hermione hide out at 12 Grimmauld Place. There they meet up with both house-elves, Dobby and Kreacher. Even though the actors who voiced them would not be seen in the film, they acted out the entire scene on the set so the animators could catch the way they looked at each other and their physical interactions. Then the scene was done again with actors of short stature playing the roles. This helped the other actors who no longer had to look at a tennis ball! The actors playing Dobby and Kreacher were covered in grey outfits that had reference points placed on them to help the animators maintain their positions during the scene. Then the computer artists used all these performances as reference for creating the house-elves.

OLD FRIENDS

For their last appearances in the film series, in *Harry Potter and the Deathly Hallows – Part 1*, the director and visual-effects team felt that the audience needed to have more of an emotional connection with Dobby and even Kreacher. They were 'humanised', in that their features were softened and as several years had passed, they were made to look older.

"*Dobby has no master! Dobby is a free elf, and Dobby has come to save Harry Potter and his friends!*"

– DOBBY, HARRY POTTER AND THE DEATHLY HALLOWS – PART 1

MAKEOVERS

For *Harry Potter and the Deathly Hallows – Part 1*, Dobby's arms were shortened, his neck and face were smoothed out and his eyes were reshaped to appear less saucerlike and less bulging. He is still dressed in a tea towel, but it's much cleaner and he's wearing shoes. He also had a softer, more radiant look which the filmmakers felt would make him even more sympathetic.

Kreacher also had a makeover for *Deathly Hallows – Part 1*, with the team making his skin smoother as well and reducing the size of his nose. They also trimmed his ear hair.

A BEAUTIFUL PASSING

The only time a full Dobby model was used in filming was in *Harry Potter and the Deathly Hallows – Part 1*, when Harry holds the dying Dobby in his arms. Dobby's death on the beach at Shell Cottage involved not only the life-size model and the CGI version of the character but also a real-life body double who performed in the scene. This was not Toby Jones, however, because he's much taller, so they used a person of short stature. When Dobby passes away, the visual-effects designers made his eyes watery and slowly changed the texture of his skin to make him appear paler and paler.

SOULFUL PERFORMANCE

"People had to really feel sympathetic when Dobby dies in *Harry Potter and the Deathly Hallows – Part 1,*" says senior visual-effects supervisor Tim Burke. "If Dobby didn't look like he had a soul, we would have lost that sadness at the end of the film. Toby Jones gave us a brilliant performance to reference, and then the excellent animators rendered a highly emotional moment just beautifully."

FILLING IN

The person of short stature who played Dobby at the Shell Cottage location was actually slightly larger than the animated house-elf. When the special-effects wizards reviewed the film footage that was shot, they found that the actor had covered much of Daniel Radcliffe's body when he picked up and carried Dobby. So the team filmed references of Daniel's arms and hands, and the jacket and shirt he wore, and then recreated them digitally to fill in the gaps.

"Such a beautiful place to be with friends. Dobby is happy to be with his friend Harry Potter."

– DOBBY, HARRY POTTER AND THE
DEATHLY HALLOWS – PART 1

A PERFECT END

The death of Dobby is a very strong, emotional scene, and the filmmakers thought that this was the best way to end the film. "After several ideas, we realised that we should end it with the burial of Dobby," says director David Yates, "which enforces Harry's commitment to carry on and find the means with which to defeat the Dark Lord, no matter what." To emphasise Harry's strong connection to Dobby, Harry chooses to bury him properly by hand, without the use of magic. Actor Daniel Radcliffe thought it was fitting and right. "Harry wants to invest as much love in Dobby's burial as Dobby showed him throughout his life," he explains.

HERE
LIES
DOBBY
A
FREE ELF

MAKE IT YOUR OWN

One of the great things about IncrediBuilds™ models is that each one is completely customisable. The untreated natural wood can be decorated with paints, pencils, pens, beads, sequins – the list goes on and on!

Before you start building and decorating your model though, read through the included instruction sheet so you understand how all the pieces fit together. Then, choose a theme and make a plan. Do you want to make an exact replica of Dobby or something completely different? Why not try matching Dobby's pillowcase to the colours of your favourite Hogwarts house? The choice is yours! Here is an example to get those creative juices flowing.

TIPS BEFORE YOU BEGIN

* As a general rule of thumb, you'll want to use pens and pencils *before* building the model and paints *after* building the model.

* When making a replica, it's always good to study an actual image of what you are trying to copy. Look closely at details and brainstorm how you can recreate them.

PAINTING DOBBY

1. For Dobby, it is very helpful to paint certain pieces before fully assembling the model. To start, paint the assembled head piece **just after step 7 in the instructions.** Choose a main colour that comes close to matching the house-elf's skin colour. Then, after applying a base coat of that colour, fill in the details of his face, such as the eyes.

2. Next, using the same base colour you did for Dobby's face, paint both arms. Make sure you leave the tab at the shoulder blank. This will make it easier to attach the arms to the body.

3. **Continue building to step 18.** Now paint Dobby's pillowcase. A neutral colour was used here to reflect Dobby's actual clothes in the film.

4. **Next, paint the legs after step 20.** After Dobby is completely assembled, you can add more details.

5. Using a rough dry brush, dab the pillowcase with a darker colour. You don't need much paint to give the pillowcase a worn-out look. Experiment with it. If you don't like the effect, you can always paint over it!

6. For Dobby's body, paint a few small grey lines. Smudge the lines with your finger or brush to complete Dobby's hard-working look.

IncrediBuilds™
A Division of Insight Editions LP
PO Box 3088
San Rafael, CA 94912
www.insighteditions.com

Find us on Facebook: www.facebook.com/InsightEditions

Follow us on Twitter: @insighteditions

ISBN: 978-1-68298-005-7

Publisher: Raoul Goff
Art Director: Chrissy Kwasnik
Designer: Jenelle Wagner
Executive Editor: Vanessa Lopez
Project Editor: Greg Solano
Production Editor: Elaine Ou
Production Coordinator: Sam Taylor
Model Designer: Ryan Zhang

INSIGHT EDITIONS would like to thank Victoria Selover, Melanie Swartz, Elaine
Piechowski, Ashley Bol, Margo Guffin, George Valdiviez, and Kevin Morris.

ART CREDITS: Dobby concept art of Rob Bliss, Adam Brockbank, and various
other artists; Kreacher concept art by Rob Bliss; Winky concept art by
Dermot Power.

Manufactured in China

iSeek Ltd, 1A Stairbridge Court, Bolney Grange Business Park,
Haywards Heath, RH17 5PA, UK